Dachshunds

Sarah Frank

Lerner Publications • Minneapolis

Lerner Publications Company
A division of Lerner Publishing Group, Inc.
241 First Avenue North
Minneapolis, MN 55401 USA

For reading levels and more information, look up this title at www.lernerbooks.com.

Library of Congress Cataloging-in-Publication Data

Names: Frank, Sarah, author.
Title: Dachshunds / Sarah Frank.
Description: Minneapolis : Lerner Publications, [2019] | Series: Lightning bolt books. who's a good dog? | Audience: Ages 6–9. | Audience: K to Grade 3. | Includes bibliographical references and index.
Identifiers: LCCN 2018035862 (print) | LCCN 2018037592 (ebook) | ISBN 9781541556645 (eb pdf) | ISBN 9781541555747 (lb : alk. paper)
Subjects: LCSH: Dachshunds—Juvenile literature. | Dogs—Juvenile literature.
Classification: LCC SF429.D25 (ebook) | LCC SF429.D25 F73 2019 (print) | DDC 636.753/8—dc23

LC record available at https://lccn.loc.gov/2018035862

Manufactured in the United States of America
1-46029-43352-11/28/2018

Table of Contents

Hot Dog!

Is that a walking hot dog? No, it's a dachshund! Dachshunds are also sometimes called wiener dogs.

Dachshunds come in two sizes. Bigger dachshunds weigh up to 32 pounds (14 kg). The smaller dogs weigh 11 pounds (5 kg) or less.

Some dachshunds have short, smooth coats. Others have long hair. Still others are called wirehaired. Their coats have a rougher feel.

Which coat do you like best?

All dachshunds are alert, smart, and loyal. It's no wonder their owners love them!

Little Hunters

The American Kennel Club (AKC) groups dogs by breed. Dachshunds are in the hound group. Hound dogs make fantastic hunters.

What do dachshunds hunt? Originally, they hunted badgers. The long, thin dogs could easily fit in badger holes.

Badgers make holes in the ground for shelter.

Some dachshunds still live on farms.

Dachshunds come from Germany. German farmers loved them. Dachshunds stopped badgers from eating farm crops.

In the nineteenth century, many Germans moved to the United States. They brought their dachshunds with them. The pooches soon became very popular in their new country.

Dachshunds remain popular family pets.

Your Kind of Dog?

Are you a dachshund person? These dogs are great, but they aren't for everyone. Your family can help you decide if you should bring a dachshund puppy home.

Dachshunds dig. They've been known to dig up yards and lawns. If your family has a vegetable garden, you might not want a dachshund.

Short daily walks are enough exercise for dachshunds.

Do you love to go on all-day hikes? Don't expect your dachshund to join you. A big, strong German shepherd might be a better fit if you're super active.

Do you have younger brothers or sisters? Make sure they can be gentle with your dog. A dachshund's long back is easily hurt. Don't get a dachshund if you can't be really careful.

You must be very gentle if you're going to have a dachshund.

Coming Home

Does your family still want a dachshund? Then it's time to buy supplies! Your dog will need bowls, toys, and a leash.

You'll also want to take your pet to a vet. The vet will check your dog's health. Your dog may need shots too.

Your dachshund needs a good diet. Choose a good-quality dog food. Ask your vet what's best.

Your dachshund will be a true friend. Be there for your dog, and she'll be there for you. That's the long and short of owning a dachshund.

Doggone Good Tips!

- Wondering what to name your new dog? Here are some ideas: Lovey, Dash, Doxie, Skiddoo, Oscar, or Schnoodle.

- A wiry coat isn't the only thing that makes wirehaired dachshunds special. These dogs also have beards!

- Keep your dachshund on a leash. Most modern dachshunds don't hunt much, but they still like to chase things. If your dachshund sees a squirrel, he may be off and running.

Why Dachshunds Are the Best

- Some heroic dachshunds work as therapy dogs. Their owners bring them to nursing homes or hospitals. The friendly dogs make the patients feel better.

- Many famous people love dachshunds. The artist Pablo Picasso, the singer Madonna, and the author E. B. White all had dachshunds as pets.

- Dachshunds look great in costume. Their owners have dressed them as princesses, pirates, and—of course—hot dogs!

Glossary

alert: aware and ready to act

American Kennel Club (AKC): an organization that groups dogs by breed

breed: a particular kind of dog

coat: a dog's hair

hound group: a group of dogs that tend to have good noses and make good hunters

loyal: showing support for a person

vet: a doctor who treats animals

Further Reading

American Kennel Club (AKC)
https://www.akc.org

American Society for the Prevention of Cruelty to Animals
https://www.aspca.org

Fishman, Jon M. *Hero Therapy Dogs*. Minneapolis: Lerner Publications, 2017.

Gray, Susan H. *Dachshunds*. New York: AV2 by Weigl, 2017.

Schuh, Mari. *Dachshunds*. Minneapolis: Bellwether Media, 2016.

Index

Photo Acknowledgments

Image credits: Alena.Kravchenko/Shutterstock.com, pp. 2, 15; SkaLd/Shutterstock.com, p. 4; ch_ch/Shutterstock.com, p. 5; DarioEgidi/Getty Images, p. 6; YakobchukOlena/Getty Images, p. 7; dageldog/Getty Images, p. 8; Coatesy/Shutterstock.com, p. 9; Luminoisty-images.com/Shutterstock.com, p. 10; Sappington Todd/Getty Images, p. 11; Ermolaev Alexander/Shutterstock.com, p. 12; Denis Babenko/Shutterstock.com, p. 13; JMichl/Getty Images, p. 14; Bulltus_casso/Shutterstock.com, p. 16; Allison Michael Orenstein/Getty Images, p. 17; Peter Vernon Morris/Shutterstock.com, p. 18; Tatyana Vyc/Shutterstock.com, p. 19; Nikolai Tsvetkov/Shutterstock.com, p. 22; cynoclub/Shutterstock.com, p. 23.

Cover Image: zhao hui/Getty Images

Main body text set in Billy Infant regular 28/36. Typeface provided by SparkType.